SKILLED AND VOCATIONAL TRADES

BECOME A PARALEGAL

by Amy C. Rea

BrightPoint Press

San Diego, CA

BrightPoint Press

an imprint of ReferencePoint Press, Inc.
Printed in the United States

For more information, contact:
BrightPoint Press
PO Box 27779
San Diego, CA 92198
www.BrightPointPress.com

LIBRARY OF CONGRESS CATALOGING-IN-PUBLICATION DATA

Name: Rea, Amy C., author.
Title: Become a paralegal / by Amy C. Rea.
Description: San Diego, CA: ReferencePoint Press, 2027 | Series: Skilled and vocational trades | Includes bibliographical references and index. | Audience: Grades 7–9
Identifiers: ISBN 9781678214647 (hardcover) | ISBN 9781678214654 (eBook)
The complete Library of Congress record is available at www.loc.gov.

CONTENTS

AT A GLANCE

- A paralegal works with lawyers. Paralegals are not lawyers themselves.
- Paralegals have many responsibilities. They do legal research, write legal documents, and communicate with lawyers' clients.
- Paralegals used to be trained on the job. They did not need to have legal education or experience.
- Today, more paralegals are expected to have paralegal certificates or college degrees.
- Paralegals usually work Monday through Friday during the day. Sometimes they are expected to work longer or on weekends.
- Paralegals need to have strong research, communication, and writing skills.

- A paralegal's day can be busy. It can also change often as a lawyer's needs change or new tasks arise.
- The paralegal field is expected to hold steady without much growth. But some paralegals will retire or change jobs, and new paralegals will take those jobs.
- Technology has become an important part of a paralegal's job. They need to continue to use new technology, including artificial intelligence.

A DAY AS A PARALEGAL

Nina arrives at her paralegal job. It is early in the morning. But she has a lot to do.

Nina works at a law firm. This is a place that handles legal cases. These are arguments between people or businesses in a court. The case determines whether a person or business is guilty of a crime. It can also decide whether one party owes another money.

Paralegals are part of the legal field.

Nina has a busy day planned. One of the lawyers she works for is handling a medical lawsuit. He needs her to find his client's medical records. She must also find the client's bills.

She gets to her desk. She checks her email. She learns that a different lawyer has a new task for her. It needs to be done right away. There was a car crash during the night. Some people were injured. Nina needs to help the lawyer put together a case.

Nina finds news stories that reported the accident. Then she looks for buildings that may have caught the accident on their security cameras. Security cameras do not always keep videos for a long time. So Nina must find the videos as soon as possible.

Many paralegals work in offices. But others work from home.

That work takes most of the morning. Nina can finally begin her medical research. But then another lawyer interrupts. He asks her to put together exhibits for a **trial** that starts soon. Nina already created a folder to keep records for the exhibit. Now she must go through it. She has to decide which records should be presented.

Paralegals often handle many cases, so they must be organized.

It is midafternoon before she starts the medical research. But she does not mind the change to her plans. Her job is interesting. It is always changing. She never knows what the day will bring. But she likes knowing that she is helping people.

PARALEGALS

Paralegals work for lawyers. They help lawyers research. They also help build legal cases.

Paralegals research topics that affect legal cases. They might research laws. Others research science. They sometimes find experts. The experts then speak at trials.

Paralegals write legal documents. They also communicate with lawyers' clients. These tasks may take many hours. Paralegals do this time-consuming work. This lets lawyers focus on the details of their cases. Paralegals do important legal work.

WHAT DOES A PARALEGAL DO?

Lawyers are not the only people who work in law. There is another important role in a law firm. Paralegals help lawyers with their cases.

A paralegal's role varies depending on the needs of their law firm. Their work depends on what type of law their law firm **practices**. Many law firms work in specific types of law. Other law firms have

Law firms employ many types of workers, including lawyers, paralegals, legal assistants, bookkeepers, and more.

several departments. Each department focuses on one type of law.

WHAT PARALEGALS CAN DO

Paralegals help lawyers with legal work. Lawyers work with people to solve problems through the courts. There are many kinds of problems people need legal help with. Paralegals help lawyers do their jobs.

Judi Maier is a lawyer. She also teaches paralegals. She says, "People go into the paralegal field because they see it as a way to help people resolve problems in their lives—whether it's business problems, personal problems, or criminal issues."[1]

A paralegal's job changes depending on where they work. But there are some

Some lawyers and paralegals help clients without charging money. This is called pro bono work.

responsibilities that most paralegals have. One common task is research.

Legal research is needed in every area of law. Research can take many hours. Lawyers need paralegals to research previous cases. They need paralegals to review court rulings. Paralegals have to research state laws. They must also

Paralegals write many types of documents, including contracts, legal briefs, and requests for people to appear in court or provide documents.

research **federal** laws. This research helps lawyers build their cases. It helps them decide how to respond to other lawyers. It also helps them decide how to answer questions from judges.

Paralegals often help lawyers prepare for trials. Research is part of this preparation. Paralegals also help organize evidence. They make sure lawyers have all the necessary documents.

Sometimes paralegals interview witnesses. A witness is someone who has information about a case. A paralegal may talk with witnesses. They record the discussions. The lawyer can use the recordings as evidence.

Other common paralegal tasks include creating files. Paralegals must write documents. They must also manage these documents.

Paralegals also write contracts. They manage communication with clients. Sometimes they write legal briefs. These are documents that explain what cases are about.

WHAT PARALEGALS CANNOT DO

Paralegals have many responsibilities. But there are also tasks that paralegals cannot do. They are not lawyers. They cannot give legal advice. This is when a lawyer recommends that someone take a certain legal step.

Paralegals cannot accept cases. They cannot handle cases alone. They also cannot present cases in court. Paralegals can help lawyers prepare for their cases. But a paralegal cannot take a lawyer's place.

Paralegals do not have the same privileges that lawyers have. This is because

Law school typically lasts 3 years. This is after getting a 4-year college degree.

paralegals usually do not have as much education as lawyers. Most have not been to law school. They also have not taken the bar exam. This is a test a lawyer must pass to be able to practice law. Paralegals also lack the training that lawyers have.

But that does not mean paralegals do not know much about law. Keegan Albarn is a paralegal. "It's not that a paralegal doesn't know the law or understand different legal documents," he writes. "It's that a paralegal has not passed a bar exam, and only those who pass the bar exam are allowed to give legal advice."[2]

Specialties

A paralegal can choose to specialize. This means that they choose one type of law to focus on. Paralegals have many options to choose from. Some specialize in family law. Others specialize in data privacy. Still others work in environmental law. Specializing can make paralegals more valuable. Paralegals who specialize are considered experts in their specialties. That helps them find jobs more quickly. They may also earn higher salaries.

WHO PARALEGALS WORK WITH

Paralegals work under the **supervision** of licensed lawyers. They also work with other legal staff. This includes other paralegals.

Most paralegals work in law offices. But some work for the government. Others work in companies that have strict legal requirements. These include companies that work in finance. They also include insurance companies. Large companies also often have legal departments. Paralegals work in these departments. They assist **corporate** lawyers.

WHAT TRAINING DO PARALEGALS NEED?

There are many ways to start a career as a paralegal. Many paralegals used to begin without any legal training. Law firms trained them on the job. But that has changed. Now many employers want their paralegals to have some training.

Law firms often want to hire educated paralegals. Some may require employees to have college degrees. Others require

Paralegal training and courses prepare people to succeed in their careers.

employees to go through paralegal certificate courses.

PARALEGAL CERTIFICATES

A paralegal certificate course is a class. It is focused on paralegal work. The class ends with a test. Each student who passes receives a certificate of completion.

Many schools offer these courses. Paralegal associations may also offer these certificates. Getting this certificate takes less time than getting a traditional college degree. It also costs less money.

The National Federation of Paralegal Associations (NFPA) has two programs that award students with certification. This means a student receives more than a certificate showing they completed the course. They also earn the right to have the certification listed as part of their job title.

One of the NFPA's courses is the Paralegal CORE Competency Exam (PCCE).

The Paralegal CORE Competency Exam tests people on their knowledge of ethics, contracts, and several types of law.

People must have some paralegal experience or education before being eligible to take the PCCE.

A person who passes the exam can list the certificate after their job title. Their title will say, “Paralegal, PCCE.” That helps future employers know that they have earned their certification. NFPA certifications require paralegals to take ongoing courses throughout their career. Those who do not continue taking courses lose the right to put their certifications in their job titles.

Certification is not required for US paralegals. But some employers may require it. In 2025, there were legal organizations in some states discussing making paralegal certification required. That means someday people may have to be certified to work as paralegals.

Some certificate programs welcome all students. But others require each student to have completed at least a 2-year degree. Certificates are useful for people who have degrees in subjects unrelated to law. It lets those people learn about being paralegals. But they do not have to get additional degrees. Certificates are also helpful for people who have some experience working in law.

Jessie Foss did not have a college degree when she began working at a law firm. Her first job was answering phones. She also did paperwork. She enjoyed the work. She was eventually promoted to

American Bar Association

The American Bar Association (ABA) works with people with legal careers. The ABA certifies paralegal degree programs. It also certifies certificate programs. Certified programs must meet the ABA's guidelines. The guidelines include how long a program should be. The guidelines also explain who is qualified to teach. But that does not mean other programs are not good. A student interested in a non-ABA program should research the program. They can decide if it fits their needs.

office manager. But she wanted to learn more. She wanted to be a paralegal.

"As I was doing the work, I was very curious and wanted to know more," Foss says. "So I was proactive in asking questions and getting information from the attorneys."[3] She signed up for a paralegal certificate program. Her job experience and certificate helped her get a job as a paralegal. Now she specializes in personal injury trial law.

COLLEGE DEGREES

Companies often require paralegals to have college degrees. Some require each employee to have an associate degree. This degree usually takes 2 years to earn. Others require each employee to have a bachelor's degree. This degree usually takes 4 years to earn.

A person's degree does not have to be related to law. Often people have degrees in business. Others might have degrees in government.

Some college degrees focus on paralegal studies. People can get associate degrees in paralegal studies. These degrees are offered by **community colleges**.

Community college degrees are good options for people interested in becoming paralegals. They take less time to earn than bachelor's degrees. They also cost less money. Some employers require paralegals to have these degrees to apply for jobs.

Four-year schools also offer paralegal degrees. Students take several paralegal courses. The paralegal studies part of the degree is more detailed than in the associate degree. The schools also cover general education topics. These topics include English and math.

More companies are requiring candidates to have college degrees before applying

Paralegal degree programs teach people to communicate and research. They also teach people about law.

Paralegals help lawyers with every step of the legal process.

for paralegal jobs. So having a degree in paralegal studies can make finding a job easier. A paralegal with a college degree may also earn more money than other paralegals.

Randy Rubin is a lawyer. He says he prefers to hire paralegals with more training. “In the past, it’s been extremely difficult to even get applicants who had basic computer skills, let alone knowledge of the court system,” he says. “We don’t worry about that when they come from [a college].”[4]

CHAPTER THREE

WHAT IS LIFE LIKE AS A PARALEGAL?

A paralegal's tasks vary depending on where they work. The exact tasks they do depend on their employer. Tasks may also vary depending on whether a paralegal is a specialist.

Nearly 75 percent of paralegals work at law firms. The remaining 25 percent of paralegals work for the government or corporations. Paralegals in these fields may have very different types of work.

In 2024, the median salary for paralegals was $61,010.

Paralegals often have more regular hours than lawyers.

Jobs can also vary depending on a company's size. Some paralegals work for large companies. These companies hire many paralegals. Each paralegal often specializes in one type of law. They have certain work requirements. These requirements will be different than those of a paralegal at a smaller law firm. These law firms hire fewer paralegals. So they must work with many kinds of law.

Different organizations also require different work. A paralegal working at a corporation will focus on certain areas of law. A paralegal working for a criminal justice lawyer will focus on other areas. But there are things most paralegals do.

TYPICAL HOURS AND WORKDAYS

Most paralegals work Monday through Friday. Office hours are usually 9:00 a.m. to 5:00 p.m. Those are the same hours that courts are open. But there are times when a paralegal will have to work later. Other times they may have to work over the weekend.

A paralegal's time is divided into two categories. Billable hours are hours spent working for a client. The client is expected to pay for the paralegal's time spent on their case. That includes time the paralegal spends researching the case. It also includes the time they spend preparing for trial. Lawyers also have billable hours. But their billing rates are higher than paralegal rates.

Non-billable hours include tasks that are not directly related to a case. That includes office meetings. It also includes training. This time is paid for by the law firm.

EMPLOYEE OR FREELANCER

Most paralegals are employees. That means a company has hired them to work. They usually receive a salary. They can also earn benefits. Benefits include

In 2022, 5 percent of paralegals were freelancers.

medical insurance. They might also include paid vacation time.

Freelance paralegals work for themselves. Law firms and other companies hire freelance paralegals to help lawyers. But the paralegals are not permanent employees of the company. Freelance paralegals sign contracts with companies. These documents determine how much they will be paid. There are usually no additional benefits. The contracts may be ongoing. They may also be based on specific projects or cases. These contracts usually end when the projects are over.

There are many benefits to being an employee. Employees have steady jobs.

Paralegals usually need to have experience before starting successful freelancing careers.

They do not have to find clients on their own. Employees receive regular paychecks. They get benefits. This includes insurance. It also includes paid time off.

Freelance paralegals have to find companies to work for. They can decide what projects they want to accept. They can decide how much work they want to do. But they will have to get their own insurance. And they do not get paid when they take time off.

PARALEGAL SKILLS

Successful paralegals need to develop several strong skills. One of their big tasks is research. They need to research many topics. They have to understand laws. They have to research medical information.

Paralegals do different types of research. Their work depends on what their lawyers need.

Paralegals must also be good at communicating. They must communicate with clients. Sometimes they interview witnesses. They write a wide variety of legal documents.

Flexibility is Key

It is important for a paralegal to be flexible. They must be able to handle changes quickly. Jeffrey Hauck is a professor of criminal justice and paralegal studies. He says, "Understand that it is a [changing] profession where you will be dealing with **novel** challenges on a daily basis, ensuring that each will usually be different."

Jeffrey Hauck, "4 Career Insights: A Day in the Life of a Paralegal," Blackstone Career Institute, *July 5, 2023. https://blackstone.edu.*

Paralegals also use communication skills at meetings. Lawyers often have paralegals attend events. These events include readings of wills. These are documents that explain what happens to someone's property after they die.

A TYPICAL DAY

A paralegal's day is busy. They often start their day with a plan. But they may find they have to change course quickly. "I typically work 8 hours a day," says Kayla Basenese. She is a paralegal. She works at a law office. "And the environment is fast-paced and constantly changing," she says.[5]

A paralegal's day often involves legal research. They use many tools to help them research. Paralegals often use special

WHERE PARALEGALS AND LEGAL ASSISTANTS WORK

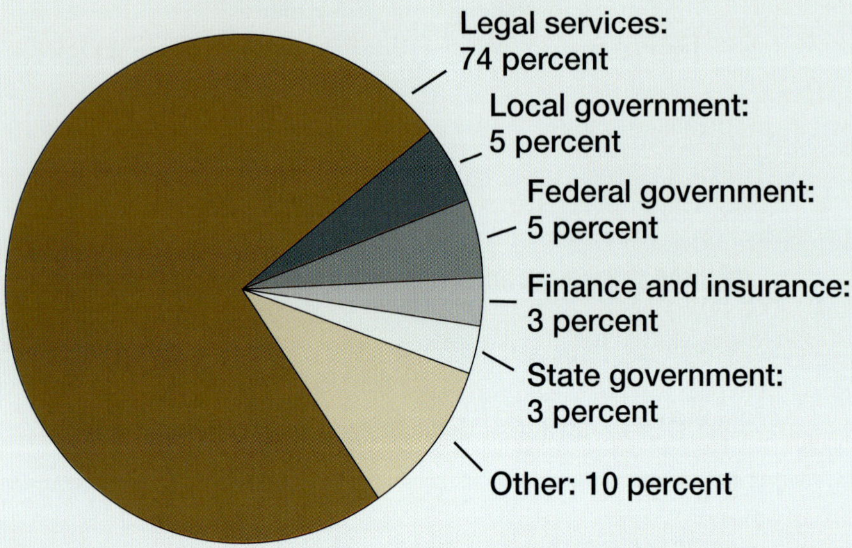

Source: "Paralegals and Legal Assistants," US Bureau of Labor Statistics, *August 28, 2025. www.bls.gov.*

Most paralegals work for lawyers in law offices. But there are other places paralegals can work.

legal databases. These databases have information about all aspects of national law. Paralegals may also read newspapers. Some read law books. They may search the internet to find the information they need.

Paralegals also spend time talking to or emailing clients about their cases.

A paralegal may be expected to manage a lawyer's court schedule. They must keep the lawyer informed of any changes. Paralegals often do office manager tasks in smaller firms. This may include paying bills. It may also include organizing records.

CHAPTER FOUR

WHAT IS THE FUTURE FOR PARALEGALS?

The paralegal career is relatively new. Lawyers learned they needed help with their cases. They also needed a way to reduce costs for their clients. Working with someone who was not a lawyer but could do writing and research filled those needs.

The idea caught on. Paralegal programs started offering courses in the late 1960s. Much has changed in the profession since then. Technology changed the way

Some people work as paralegals with the goal of eventually becoming lawyers.

paralegals work. Paralegals used to file documents in person. But they can now do this online. This is called e-filing.

Former paralegal Ann Pearson says, "I'm glad that paralegals are no longer driving to the clerk's office to file paper pleadings

Law firms, health care organizations, real estate firms, and government agencies all hire paralegals.

and motions or to research things. Before e-filing, it was nothing for a paralegal to be watching the clock as the attorney finished that brief [and] calculating where to find parking."[6] The paralegal career is expected to continue changing in the years ahead.

CAREER OUTLOOK FOR PARALEGALS

The Bureau of Labor Statistics (BLS) is a government department. It tracks information about jobs. It predicts whether different career paths will grow or slow down. The BLS says that there were more than 376,000 paralegals and legal assistants working in the United States in 2024. The BLS predicts that number will remain steady through 2034.

The field is not expected to grow. But that does not mean there will not be jobs available. The BLS says that about 40,000 people leave their paralegal and legal assistant jobs each year. Some will retire. Others will pursue different jobs. They may try different paralegal jobs or branch out into a different career. Their jobs can be filled by new paralegals.

PARALEGAL TRENDS

Paralegal careers will likely change in the future. Specializing will likely become more important. Paralegals who focus on one area of law may find jobs faster. Paralegals who specialize in **cybersecurity** could be in demand. People who work in this area stop technology from being hacked.

Paralegals must be skilled with using computers.

Law firms may also need paralegals who specialize in **artificial intelligence (AI)**.

Technology has changed how paralegals work. Paralegals no longer have to go to courthouses to file or collect documents. Much of their work can be done on their computers. But that raises concerns about data privacy. Paralegals will need to learn more about online privacy. They must know how to protect their clients' information.

Paralegal careers started out as something a person could learn on the job. That has changed. It may change even more. New paralegals may need to have advanced education to enter this

Paralegals and AI

AI can help lawyers and paralegals do their jobs. But it cannot replace them. Not all of what AI does is correct. Paralegals need to verify what AI tells them. Johnnathan Ruff is a paralegal. He says, "Technology is not replacing paralegals but empowering them to become more adaptable and efficient."

Johnnathan S. Ruff, "From Typewriters to Tablets: Navigating Technological Advancements for Paralegals – Q2 2025 Facts & Findings," National Association of Legal Assistants, *2025. https://nala.org.*

career path. It is possible that paralegals will be required to have specialized training in the future.

SUPPORT FOR NEW PARALEGALS

New paralegals used to have few resources to support them. But that is changing. There are now professional organizations for paralegals. A professional organization is a group of people who have similar careers. They meet to share information. They can also share resources with each other.

There are several national paralegal organizations. One is the NFPA. Another is the National Association of Legal Assistants/ Paralegal Association. Both offer education. They also provide training. They offer ways to meet other paralegals. Some states

Members of the National Association of Legal Assistants/Paralegal Association receive educational opportunities, career help, and more.

and larger cities also have paralegal associations. This allows paralegals to meet nearby people in the same careers.

Many programs have teachers who used to work as lawyers or paralegals. This gives paralegal students the opportunity to learn from someone who works in law. Law firms may also offer mentors to new paralegals.

A mentor is someone who advises another person.

MORE DIVERSE PARALEGAL WORKFORCE

In 2023, half of the people who earned paralegal degrees were white. About 23 percent were Hispanic or Latino. Roughly 14 percent were Black. About 3 percent were Asian. Less than 1 percent were Indigenous.

Many companies are working to make the paralegal workforce more diverse. These employers are **recruiting** people from underrepresented groups. Employers attend job fairs focused on minority applicants. Some have diversity committees. These groups

In 2020, roughly 85 percent of paralegals were women.

create plans for hiring employees from diverse backgrounds.

Paralegals are less well known than lawyers and judges. But they do very important work. They help lawyers build cases. They connect with clients. And they do important research. Lawyers will continue to rely on paralegals for important law firm work. And soon a new generation of workers will step in to join the career.

GLOSSARY

artificial intelligence (AI)

technology that can do complex tasks that only humans used to be able to do

community colleges

schools that offer educational programs, often 2-year programs and certificates, in specific areas of study

corporate

relating to a company or business

federal

relating to the national government

novel

new

practices

does or carries out

recruiting

seeking out new employees

supervision

the oversight of another

trial

a case heard in a court of law

SOURCE NOTES

CHAPTER ONE: WHAT DOES A PARALEGAL DO?

1. Quoted in "How to Become a Paralegal," *Professional & Continuing Education University of Washington*, May 24, 2023. www.pce.uw.edu.

2. Keegan Albarn, "What Paralegals Can and Cannot Do (and What They Shouldn't)," *KA Paralegal Schools*, n.d. https://kaparalegalschools.com.

CHAPTER TWO: WHAT TRAINING DO PARALEGALS NEED?

3. Quoted in Ann Pearson, "Starting a Paralegal Career Without a Paralegal Certificate," *Paralegal Bootcamp*, April 28, 2023. https://paralegal-bootcamp.com.

4. Quoted in Crystal Sullivan, "Diploma in One Hand, Job in the Other," *Umpqua Community College*, n.d. https://umpqua.edu.

CHAPTER THREE: WHAT IS LIFE LIKE AS A PARALEGAL?

5. Quoted in Will Erstad, "A Day in the Life of a Paralegal: Your Curiosities Answered," *Rasmussen University*, June 6, 2023. www.rasmussen.edu.

CHAPTER FOUR: WHAT IS THE FUTURE FOR PARALEGALS?

6. Ann Pearson, "10 Things We're Glad Have Changed in the Paralegal Profession," *Paralegal Bootcamp*, June 17, 2022. https://paralegal-bootcamp.com.

FOR FURTHER RESEARCH

BOOKS

Carla Mooney, *The Government Encyclopedia*. Abdo Publishing, 2023.

Hall Rose, *Law for Beginners*. Usborne Publishing, 2021.

Daniel Sokol and Ronald Sokol, *A Young Person's Guide to Law and Justice*. Troubador Publishing, 2024.

INTERNET SOURCES

Laura Berlinsky-Schine, "How to Become a Paralegal: Steps to Take from High School," *CollegeVine*, December 13, 2020. https://blog.collegevine.com.

Imed Bouchrika, "What a Paralegal Does and How to Become One for 2025," *Research.com*, March 16, 2026. https://research.com.

Katelyn Fahrenbruck Weston, "Pros and Cons of Being a Paralegal," *U.S. Career Institute*, December 2025. www.uscareerinstitute.edu.

WEBSITES

American Bar Association: Paralegals
www.americanbar.org/topics/paralegal

The American Bar Association is one of the country's leading legal associations. It offers news and educational resources for paralegals.

The National Association of Legal Assistants
https://nala.org

The National Association of Legal Assistants is a professional organization for paralegals. The organization gives paralegals access to education, training, and certification opportunities.

Paralegal Today
www.legalassistanttoday.com

Paralegal Today is a website devoted to paralegals. It provides job listings, educational opportunities, articles about various aspects of paralegal work, and online forums for paralegals to connect with one another.

INDEX

IMAGE CREDITS

Cover: © Nansan Houn/iStockphoto
5: © William Potter/Shutterstock Images
7: © Jacob Wackerhausen/iStockphoto
9: © Korrawin/iStockphoto
10: © nirat/iStockphoto
13: © PeopleImages/Shutterstock Images
15: © Amnaj Khetsamtip/Shutterstock Images
16: © Suwatchai Wongaong/Shutterstock Images
19: © michaeljung/iStockphoto
23: © Katarzyna Bialasiewicz/iStockphoto
25: © Mangostar/Shutterstock Images
26: © Josep Suria/Shutterstock Images
31: © vm/iStockphoto
32: © Kzenon/Shutterstock Images
35: © LightField Studios/Shutterstock Images
36: © dekazigzag/Shutterstock Images
39: © PreciousJ/Shutterstock Images
40: © PanuShot/Shutterstock Images
44: Red Line Editorial
47: © AnnaStills/iStockphoto
48: © Peter Silverman Photo/Shutterstock Images
51: © Freedomz/Shutterstock Images
54: © PeopleImages/Shutterstock Images
56: © f.t.Photographer/Shutterstock Images

ABOUT THE AUTHOR

Amy C. Rea grew up in northern Minnesota and now lives in a Minneapolis suburb with her family. She writes frequently about traveling around Minnesota and loves spending time with her family and her silly dog.